Blessed Brokenness

Reverend Matthew Hogan

Published by Reverend Matthew Hogan, 2023.

BLESSED BROKENNESS

First edition. October 10, 2023.

Copyright © 2023 Reverend Matthew Hogan.

ISBN: 979-8223348856

Written by Reverend Matthew Hogan.

Table of Contents

Acknowledgments

Thank you to Mrs. Millie Samuelson for encouraging me to write and to get published.

Thank you to my gaggle of beta readers who kept me on track.

Thank you to my bride for encouraging me every day and letting me share our story.

Foreward

Already a published author in his own right, Brother Matthew continues to challenge his readers—believers and non-believers, alike.

I had the privilege of meeting Matthew decades ago, when we attended a Saturday morning men's fellowship group. Matthew was genuine then, and nothing has changed.

In his latest book, <u>Blessed Brokenness: Finding God's Glory in the Ashes of Life,</u> he challenges with every page, living the definition of vulnerability.

In "Blessed", you find a relatable author, where life's ups and downs live. He unapologetically tackles divorce, chronic pain, the death of a young sibling-and more—but doesn't *leave* us there, choosing instead to usher us up into the loving arms of a waiting Heavenly Father, where peace and provision reign.

No matter what denomination (or lack of one) you find yourself to be a part of, this work will draw you in.

Start the journey that takes you from broken — to whole.

Les Linz, author of "40 Days of Passion: Toward Greater Intimacy with your Lord", "God in the Hands of Angry Sinners, "Coping Midst Unrest: Hope from the Psalms", and more.

Preface

Honestly, this book is a labor of love. I want so much to help others that might be hurting or will be hurting to find peace. I have to admit, to get to full peace, it took some time. God knew I wasn't too happy with Him from time to time, because I wanted things my way or at least to be let in on the plan. He didn't budge.

But a little over a year before writing this preface, God got through to me. Today, although I don't like the difficult times that come, I have a newly found peace that I am just where I belong. I hope you find that same peace as you come with me on my journey.

I ask that you get your favorite Bible, as I refer to scripture, but have chosen not to include the actual text as I would greatly prefer that you read from the translation that you prefer.

Are you ready? Let's get started.

Matthew

A little help down here, please?

In 2 Corinthians 1:20 it says, "For as many as are the promises of God, in Him they are yes; therefore also through Him is our Amen to the glory of God through us."[1] But do you ever feel like that's hard to believe? I mean, "All His promises are yes," seriously? A very dear friend, a long term pastor, said to me. "Sometimes I want to scream, 'A little help down here, please'" His frustration was so clear as he practically screamed it and waved his arms up at heaven.

In my book, *How to be a Christian in Todays World: Shame or Fear of Failure vs. Living Confidently in God's Love*, I talked about how much God loves us, and if we can only see it, everything changes. But I also admitted briefly that I had to face my own mortality to begin to really understand it. I likened it to a 'bottom of the barrel' moment. But maybe it is better seen as a moment on the road to Damascus.

I say that because, for many years after I entered ministry, I continued to be in that place where what I 'knew' and 'believed' didn't always translate to what my life was saying. In other words, in church I heard and even preached how much God loved us, then came home and spent the rest of the week not understanding the correlation between what I said I believed and the pain and questions that haunted me. Whether you are there now, have been there before, or will be in the future, many of us find ourselves caught with 'what we need here and now in this life is just not feeling like the love and grace of God.' You may feel like my pastor friend; struggling, ignored, and alone.

How did I discover glory in the ashes?

The only way I can possibly relate this to you is to tell you the story. My earliest memories include or revolve around my brother.

My brother and I regularly woke before our parents. One morning he wanted to get into his wheelchair and move around on his own, but our parents weren't awake yet. Our bedrooms were upstairs and for some reason his chair was downstairs. I remember trying to push his wheelchair up the stairs when it was much bigger than I was because he wanted to get up NOW.

As young children in the early 1970s, we constantly saw Vietnam veterans coming home to a country that didn't welcome them. Too many of them were mangled and maimed and resorted to begging on the streets. My dad in particular hated begging. Since my brother was in a wheelchair, my parents made sure that we (my brother really) didn't decide to beg, using his wheelchair as an excuse. So they would preach at us, "You don't beg. You work for yourself!" I remember pushing my brother's wheelchair at Disneyland without being able to see anything but the back of his chair as he would help and steer when all of a sudden, we were surrounded by Shriners[2]. At the time, that was pretty scary for two reasons. First, we were surrounded by these men in funny-looking hats. And secondly, these Shriners were throwing stuffed animals and ticket books in my brother's lap. With the no begging rule, we were terrified of the trouble we'd be in when our parents got to us.

And I remember finding him dead one morning and much of the surreal day that followed. I gave some of the details of that morning in my *book How to be a Christian in Today's World: Shame or Fear of Failure vs. Living Confidently in God's Love*. As usual, I woke up early that morning and went in to his room to talk and play. We were the best of friends and never fought. But that morning, as soon as I walked into his room, I knew something was wrong. His head was hanging off his bed. I pushed his head back onto the bed and tried to wake him. In my young mind, there was a dichotomy. I knew he was dead, but also knew I shouldn't understand that. I went to my mom's door and stood there, afraid to wake her but desperately wanting her help. I stood there going back and forth in my mind until she came out. She ran in and started CPR and sent me across the street to have the neighbors call the fire department.

I remember my parents fighting and finally divorcing after my brother's death. That essentially left me to raise myself from the age of 10 on. So, yeah, I had what many would consider a rough childhood, though I never did. I just navigated it and dealt with it. But it helped shape me, some for good and some not so much. The not so much was that I felt very alone and lonely and was basically a jerk for a number of years.

In college, I cared for a friend's disabled son. He had severe/profound disabilities, being non-verbal with very little muscle coordination. For some reason, I was the only one my friend would trust him with, so I spent a good amount of time with him. Between my brother and this young man, I became very comfortable being around people with disabilities.

When I met a cute girl in line for an Allies[3] concert, I didn't really notice her limp and the arm that sometimes curled up. All I saw was that this new girl I met was gorgeous and paid attention to me! A short time later, we married.

A pause in the story for what we are taught and maybe believe

My Christian background is very diverse. I've ministered in liturgical churches; attended a fundamentalist college; and spent many years attending and ministering in charismatic churches; and even a reformed church (if you are unfamiliar with these terms, just know that the differences in doctrine and teaching are extensive). How theology surrounding the Holy Spirit is understood and taught is a key difference. Some believe that the Holy Spirit isn't active today whereas the other end of the spectrum believes that a true Christian life and suffering are mutually exclusive. Some of the latter group believe that if you are sick or poor, there must be something wrong in your faith life or understanding. My personal perspective falls somewhere in the middle. Therefore, I will simply share my story without attempting to convince anyone or delve into those contentious issues. But what I have to say is the truth, completely, as I have lived it.

That beautiful woman I married? Well, neither of us had any idea what life would truly be like with her disability. We only knew what it was. In the early days of our marriage, she would often fall, and we simply accepted it as part of our reality. She was undergoing what were then considered experimental surgeries, which have now become the standard for individuals with her condition. During most of those surgeries, I would feel excited because I believed in the optimistic promises given by the doctor, a highly reputable professional who had earned our trust through years of caring for her and consistently improving her mobility and alleviating her pain.

We faced struggles, mostly within ourselves and as a couple, but we never really worried about anything. No matter what challenges life threw our way, we simply adapted and moved on.

The reason I share my childhood and early married life with you is to highlight that, despite all of those obstacles, we experienced very little suffering.

What is suffering?

I apologize for interrupting the story with these clarifications. It is crucial however that we are on the same page, so I need to shed some light on human nature and individual thought. Perspective plays a huge role in how we perceive whether God is taking care of us or not.

I don't know how my parents felt during my formative years in the 1960s with two sickly children. I don't know or understand the weight of the financial burdens they carried. I know that they tried to make life as normal as possible. I know I had hard moments, but I can't look back and say I ever felt suffering, and I don't think my brother did either.

When my young wife would fall and everyone around us would panic, we just took it in stride. Even when she got hurt, it was just part of life for us. Those were times that, despite the struggles, there was very little suffering. I often explain it this way: If you have a broken leg and it really isn't bothering you, and I have a paper cut that is driving me crazy all day, then who is suffering? Obviously, me with the paper cut, not because the injury is more significant, but because the impact on the psyche and the heart is greater. That is what suffering is or isn't, how we experience whatever we are going through, such as trauma or stress, and how it impacts our heart and psyche.

This is important because I'm going to take you on a journey where I felt suffering, and how I went from feeling abandoned (or at least like God was leaving me out of the loop) to finding true peace.

My wife and I served as missionaries at a Christian drug and alcohol rehab facility, which was located on a farm atop a small hill near a tiny town. One evening, we decided to take the guys out fishing as a reward. It was a moonless night, and finding the pond proved to be quite a challenge. Just a few minutes into our fishing adventure, I heard a loud thump. It turned out my wife had taken a hard fall and was in pain. It was an unexpected incident: the person most prone to injuries with the most awkward gait managed to get caught in a single loop of barbed wire sticking out from the ground, perfectly sized for her shoe. She couldn't put any weight on her injured leg, so I rushed her to the nearest hospital.

Given the limited resources and nighttime staffing of a rural hospital, we received disheartening news, "We can't identify anything specific, but it appears to be a torn ligament that will require surgery." We had no idea how we would afford the surgery or how far we would need to travel to find a skilled surgeon, so we just didn't worry about it.

During this time, one of the program's students, who had been away from the farm when my wife got injured, was approaching graduation and filled with anxiety. His past life was marked by involvement in gangs and all the associated troubles. He believed that his only way out was through serving God, yet he also believed that God would never use someone like him. Despite knowing he was forgiven, shame had taken a powerful hold on him, skillfully manipulated by the enemy.

The day after he got back, we took all the guys to church. At the end of service, this young man spun around and asked me if I believed that if we laid hands on my wife's knee and prayed, that God would heal her. Of course I said yes. While he was praying, my wife began to giggle and then laugh. I had no idea what brought the laughter and was frankly a little put off. But then I understood! As my hand was resting directly on her knee, I felt something moving under my hand! I just knew she was being healed. Sure enough, she stood up and asked him to carry her crutches to the bus, and she walked out. She was healed! That day changed him profoundly. The worry of being stuck in the gang life was gone as he gained a new confidence in God's love for him. The last I heard of him, he was entering training to become a youth minister.

The doctor who had performed my wife's earlier surgeries had one more procedure planned for her. Her leg had always curled in. She actually walked on the side of her shoes, not the sole. We spent much money replacing barely used shoes only because I had to throw away a pair of shoes because one had a hole on the side and a pristine sole. However, this doctor had a plan to change that. He used an injection to numb the muscles as a proof of concept for the surgery. This would be the first time this specific procedure had ever been performed and the injection verified it would do what he intended. In the weeks following the injection, and after she had healed from the surgery, she walked completely normally. It was an amazing transformation.

However, I had an accident at work and was out of commission for eight months. Soon after, my wife fell at her job, undoing the positive effects of the surgery and confining her to bed for months. While I was receiving worker's compensation insurance payments, hers were denied. So, we went from having two incomes to two-thirds of one. In the midst of this, her father kindly gave us a car, though he cautioned me not to thank him as it might not turn out to be much of a favor. True enough, the car didn't take long to break down, and we endured a winter in Northern Illinois without a vehicle. I walked to physical therapy and decided to cut through the large park between our apartment and the hospital instead of going all the way around it. I pushed through thigh high snow. When I went back a few days later, I was relieved that it hadn't snowed much, and others had apparently been using my path, making it wider.

Somehow, we got through those times without much emotional drama. But that was before we ever knew what the world would consider a good life. We had each been living in chaos since long before we met. We were in such a state of need that we were clinging to God at every turn. For all the struggles in our young marriage, we wanted to be together in faith. Through those early years of hardship, we easily reveled in the glory of the Lord, because that was all we knew.

An invisible line

As I thought about the whole story that makes up this book, I knew that the earlier parts in my life were important. But I also realized as I reread it, that just because I saw the connection, it might not be obvious to everyone else. This chapter is my best attempt at helping the reader understand the difference in my wife and I from the early years to the later years, and maybe a peek at something that makes deep faith so hard for so many.

In my earliest years, the chaos was normal because it was all I knew. Later, when my wife and I went through poverty and pain, we benefitted by what I've called the fortune of brokenness. We were old enough now and had seen what other people had. We had been tempted to dream of what we wanted. The simplicity of just not knowing any better didn't exist anymore. That wall of protection was gone. But the continual pain of some sort kept us in a place where we relied on God. We relied on God because we had to, we knew we couldn't survive without Him.

There's a line between those that rely on God for their very survival and those that don't have any true deep needs. I have a good friend that built two Christian rehab homes in Mexico. Carlos took me down to preach at a chapel service at one of them. We were in northern Baja. We were trying to get down to the other rehab home in southern Baja. It was during an unusual time. The recent re-arrest and extradition to the United States of Joaquin "El Chapo" Guzman left the Mexican drug cartels in a power struggle and the normal peace in Baja kept together by understandings between the cartels had been shattered. While we were trying to find out if we could get safe passage to the south, Carlos told me what to expect. He said that if we made it, once I started preaching in the morning, I'd better be ready to preach well into the night. He explained that once arrangements were made, word would spread through the villages and countryside. People from these poor villages would wake before dawn and walk several hours to have "church." These are people that know that without the grace of God, they would starve. So, they reveled in hearing His Word and worshipping Him.

One Christmas, some years ago, a pastor and his family and my wife and I were all invited to be guests for dinner and games at a mutual friend's house.

It was a wonderful afternoon and evening. When it was time for goodbyes, the pastor quietly said to me, get your coat and meet me outside. Maybe it was just because he was trying to keep it quiet and between us, but he sounded very serious. I wondered, "Did I somehow offend his wife?" When we got outside, he walked me over to the rear of his old luxury sedan. He explained that he owned a Christian bookstore and was also a pastor. He said that one Sunday morning as he was getting ready for church, God made it very clear to him that he needed to hold a food drive. He didn't know why but didn't question God. So, he held a food drive for a few weeks until He believed God was saying it was enough. He continued by telling me that early that morning he was compelled to put the food in his car. Again, he had no idea why, but didn't question God. He then said to me, "You don't have any food, do you?" I replied, "How much did Keith tell you about my situation?" He asked with a blank stare what I was talking about."

He opened the enormous trunk of his car and started handing me bags of food. It completely filled the backseat and rear floorboard of my in-law's car that we had for the holidays while they were out of town. Then there was one lone big garbage bag tucked way back in the corner of the trunk. He asked, "You haven't gotten your wife anything for Christmas, have you?" Embarrassed, I practically whispered, "Well, I made her a coupon book." He reached inside and grabbed the garbage bag and said, "Go tell your wife, Merry Christmas." Inside the bag was the biggest Teddy Bear I have ever seen.

I tell that story at this point, because although we were much better off than those poor Mexican villagers, our cupboards were as empty as Old Mother Hubbard's. And we were at a point where we had no choice but to trust God. As long as we were on that side of the invisible line, we were held by the deep fortune that comes with living in the need and assurance of God's presence and love.

Where we cross over to the other side of that invisible line is when we begin to become secure through the world. I got a good factory job and we lived with an elderly couple as evening caregivers. We had want for nothing. It didn't take long until the fortune of brokenness of that Christmas just months before was nothing but a story we shared with others. It became a "Then" and "Now." In the "Now" we no longer had to rely on God for everything, and in our society of abundance, we quickly forgot what it was like to be in that position. We were firmly on the other side of the line.

The first big challenge hit right after our sweet baby girl entered the world. We already knew that my wife needed surgery, but the doctors didn't want to take the risks of operating on a pregnant woman. I can still feel the absence of peace as I wandered through those sterile hospital hallways in Northern Illinois, holding my little bundle tight, hoping that my wife would pull through her supposedly "routine and safe" surgery. With my daughter's cries that echoed in the corridors, my own tears fell, mirroring my fear and loneliness. God's promised peace seemed miles away, and His presence felt elusive.

Just a few months later, that same little baby needed an even more minor surgery. But handing her over to the nurse, her little body limp and asleep in our arms, tore at our hearts. The whole hour or two she was gone, we kept trying not to burst into tears and asked each other at least once, "What did we do?"

My wife lived because of her surgery, and my daughter has full use of both hands because of hers. I don't feel silly about my fear then, because today, I understand what people are going through when they are in the place I once was.

In the ensuing years, my wife tried multiple times to return to work. One time she slipped and fell in a restaurant where she was working. I had to go into the back of the restaurant and carry her out. Then, in another job, she was restricting a young and violent student by holding his chair so that he couldn't attack another student. His jumping and jerking hurt her back.

Several years later, I got a phone call at work. The panicked voice said, "Your wife fell through a window and has glass sticking out of her neck." But remember, my wife fell all the time, and we became desensitized. For me, hearing that she fell meant almost nothing. Mind you, when she said that glass was sticking out of my wife's neck, I imagined those tiny little shards that you miss after sweeping up glass in the kitchen.

I drove to the school where she was teaching and saw a firetruck. No big deal; people have called fire trucks before. As I turned the corner and pulled into the school parking lot, I saw a second fire truck, "OK, that's a record." Then I saw the broken plate glass window with the middle gone and the bottom and top both looking like giant jagged teeth. I could see her shoes on the low windowsill and a parent using something to try to dry up and sweep up what looked like an enormous amount of blood on the sidewalk outside the window.

As I parked, I saw the paramedics taking the gurney inside. They seemed to be in no hurry. That had to be a really good sign or a very bad sign! A fireman grabbed me as I came through the front door. "You must be the husband. Everything's going to be fine, I'll take you to your wife."

By the time I got to her, there was no glass sticking out of her neck, but it turned out that it had been very near the jugular vein, and she and another teacher had been trying to hold it still until help arrived. They had a bandage taped to her neck, and most of the left side of her face was bandaged. Her blouse was shredded and covered in blood. Fortunately, it was brand new, and we were able to stop on the way home from the hospital and get a new one, so our daughter wouldn't be traumatized by the sight of the bloody, shredded blouse. I gradually calmed down as the very friendly and a little too handsome doctor put over 300 tiny little sutures in her face. They were hardly noticeable when we left the hospital and the scars faded beautifully.

I tell that story because I never even thought to turn to God; I was just in sheer panic as soon as I took in the whole scene at the school. That's a sobering reminder that we often don't turn to God first!

Around that time, my wife experienced significant pain on a regular basis, leading to multiple hospital visits and subsequent surgeries. Despite the challenges, she made the brave decision to pursue further education. A kind-hearted individual from the college was assigned to support her in navigating the classes and workload. However, we couldn't quite embrace the nickname she playfully gave us - Mr. and Mrs. Job. While we cherished her friendship, the label didn't work for us.

At that time in our lives, we knew that we were often an inspiration to others. We didn't understand it, but we had been told many times by enough different people that we knew it had to be true. Please understand, I don't think I or we are anything special. Somehow, God is working through our weakness! I don't begin to understand it. During that period, we realized that our experiences often served as an inspiration to others. Although we couldn't fully grasp it, we couldn't ignore how often people said something.

The beginning of a realization

A few years prior to the last chapter, my wife and I found ourselves going through a period of separation, followed by homelessness. It was a difficult and uncertain time in our lives. However, I was fortunate to have a friend who walked alongside me, providing support and even offering to store our belongings while we were without a home. As we packed up a truck, preparing to relocate to another state where the cost of living would allow us to rebuild our lives, I hugged my friend and found myself sobbing as I told him how much of a blessing he had been. He surprised me as he looked me in the eye and said, "No, you blessed me!"

I remember feeling a mix of surprise and disbelief. How could our struggles and the vulnerabilities he had witnessed throughout the toughest moments of our marriage possibly inspire him? He had seen all my flaws and witnessed the rawness of our journey. As time passed and circumstances changed, I had the opportunity to revisit the area a few years later for work. During my visit, I met up with my old friend and shared a meal together.

Over lunch, he shared profound news with me. He revealed that it was through observing our resilience and faith during our challenging times that God had used our story to call him into ministry. He had already started ministry school and later became a pastor, leading and shepherding a congregation of over 2,000 individuals. The impact of this news struck me deeply. It was awe-inspiring to think that something as personal and difficult as our journey through adversity had been instrumental in touching his life, igniting a profound transformation, and redirecting his path from a businessman to a devoted pastor.

Every time I think about it, I can't help but feel overwhelmed by the incredible blessing it is to see how God can work through the challenges we face. That we persevered amidst hardship, even with our imperfections and struggles, became a testimony that touched my friend's heart, and guided him towards a new calling. It serves as a powerful reminder of the ways in which God can use our experiences to impact and change the lives of others.

There are many more stories, and at any one point in time, some still come to mind clearly as others are hidden in obscurity. But they taught us a truth that I am only beginning to understand. You see, as we remained faithful to God and

even grew in our faith amidst the challenges, something remarkable happened –
we became a beacon of hope for those around us. Our perseverance, our ministry,
it all had a profound impact on people, whether we intended it to or not.

This truth, although we didn't dare tell anyone else about it for fear that
it would seem like bragging, actually helped us hold on in some of the darker
moments. You see, our lives, whether we wanted them to be or not, were a
ministry to people. And quite frankly, when we were hurting, we came at times
to resent what felt like a responsibility that we couldn't bear. And indeed, we
couldn't bear it. We WEREN'T strong enough and that truth holds a key that
we later came to understand.

You see, it became clear to us that our weaknesses, our vulnerabilities, held
a profound significance. It was in acknowledging our insufficiency that we
discovered the true power of God working through us. We were never meant
to rely solely on our own strength. Instead, our frailty opened the door for His
strength to shine brightly. We began to grasp the beauty in our weaknesses,
understanding that it is through them that His strength is perfected.

This revelation shifted our perspective and liberated us from the weight of
self-reliance. We recognized that our ministry was not about our own abilities
but about surrendering to God's will and allowing Him to work through us. It
was a humbling realization that continues to shape our journey.

Chronic pain haunted my wife. We couldn't or weren't willing to turn away, so we turned to God and sometimes begged Him with tears to take the pain away. There were many nights that I bravely held my wife until she cried herself to sleep. Then I begged God some more. I knew better, but I tried bargaining with Him. "If you won't just take her pain away, then give it to me!" I would lay there and try not to wake her as I begged God. I think I too, prayed and cried myself to sleep many nights.

Later on, she had a medication pump implanted under the skin, and it helped for several years. But a year before it was due to be replaced, it had a critical failure: it would sound an audible alarm for about 5 seconds every ten minutes. The crazy and most painful part of that story is that it happened within about three days of her losing her medical insurance. She had slipped through a crack between the Affordable Care Act and Medicare. It took me several months of wading through red tape to understand what had happened. I even wrote to senators and the White House. By the time I understood what had happened, the open enrollment period for Medicare had passed, and she had to wait another year to get insured.

It wasn't considered medically necessary to perform surgery to remove the pump. It would be another year before she would have surgery near the pump, so the doctor was willing to take it out while he was in the area. So, for a total of nearly 2 ½ years, we heard the alarm from the pump go off every 10 minutes. It was truly challenging at times. Then I would often fall asleep begging God that when I woke up in the morning, the pump would be laying on the bed between us. Sadly, it never happened, though I knew God could do it!

Through these challenges, we knew that God was God! That's the thing. We always had that anchor to hold on to. We knew that as frustrated and hurting as we were that God didn't do what we wanted, He still was keeping His promises. The belief that we need it our way steals joy and keeps us from seeing the beauty in all the things He has blessed us with. It's much like the illustration of a man late for an important meeting. He asked God for a parking space, and then, a car pulled out from right in front of the building where he was headed. His response? "Never mind, I found one." How much better off would we be if we were thankful to God for things He didn't do rather than the other way around? The harsh truth (this is as much a self-indictment as it is pointing the finger at anyone else) is that we often choose to be miserable when God isn't doing it our way. Yes, it IS a choice.

As I write this, my bride and I are watching one of our favorite shows, "Call the Midwife." The script, and especially the prologue and epilogue narrative, are always so excellent. As is often the case, I find my writing lacks when compared to others, whether it is my favorite preacher, musicians, or even these writers. The episode that we just watched began with a reference to the fact that no matter our belief system, we all start with the natural human need of expectation. We all look at our watches and go about our routines.

In our human brains, we naturally make thousands of assumptions every day, simply to function. For example, we assume that our chair will hold us, that the brakes will stop our car, and that when we enter an intersection on our turn to go that we will be safe. If we didn't make these assumptions, we couldn't function. Yet, the days don't always go as we expect. So many things can come and go. So much can come without warning or expectation. We would do well to remember that "This is the day that the Lord has made"[1] (Psalm 118:24). But what we are called to and verily is completely necessary to our spiritual and emotional, let alone mental survival is the end of that verse, "Rejoice and be glad in it!"[1]. Realize that this is an instruction. But it is still a choice as to whether we will obey that instruction. And maybe most importantly, this, and all the many other instructions to rejoice, are critical to our wellbeing.

About a year after I became disabled myself, a serious and significant adverse reaction to a medication created symptoms that took weeks to wear off, and nobody knew where the symptoms were coming from or if they would kill me. While hospitalized, I received my denial letter from Social Security Disability, which was no surprise as the first application is often denied. Then I got a letter from the insurance company that was due to pay my long-term disability for two more years stating that they were cancelling my payments because I no longer met their criteria as disabled. Lying in the hospital with little distraction, I imagined my wife and I trying to live out of our mid-sized crossover vehicle. I figured I could handle it. My dog could handle it. But how could I expect my paralyzed wife to live that way? Yet I knew that God would keep His promises.

Even if we were living in a car, we would still have shelter. I never doubted that we would find food. But I doubted we could keep our home on her disability check alone. So, I simultaneously knew that He would keep His promises, but I wasn't satisfied with my image of how it would happen. I could focus on His goodness and provision, knowing that He could and would likely do much more than I could imagine, or I could focus on my dissatisfaction with my imagination. I chose the latter for at least several days. Needless to say, we have a home, and He has provided beyond my wildest dreams.

"How much glory do you need?"

Following all of this, my beautiful bride then had a series of surgeries that brought evidence that she would feel better but initially continued to cause pain. And I wasn't happy with the time it was taking or not knowing how much good these surgeries would really do. The doctors all admitted that we were in unknown territory. I would lay in bed next to her or sit on the deck in the mornings and remember the man born blind. In John chapter 9, we see the story of a man that was born blind and is now an adult. Jesus healed him. It's essential to understand the prevailing cultural belief at the time, which linked physical ailments to personal sin. Even Jesus' own disciples questioned who had sinned to cause the man's blindness. Given the context, their inquiry was not unreasonable. However, Jesus responded by affirming that neither the man nor his parents were to blame for his condition. Instead, it was an opportunity for God's works to be revealed through him.

It is a common belief that the meaning of God's works being shown in this man would be to bring glory to God! The concept of God's works being revealed in the man born blind often raises the question of why someone would have to endure such a condition for the purpose of bringing glory to God. Initially, it may seem harsh or unfair. However, Matthew Henry, a renowned commentator, put forth the perspective that anyone who becomes an instrument to bring glory to God should be grateful for the opportunity. While grappling with this question personally, I too struggled to find an answer for many years. Eventually, I made the conscious decision to place my trust in the goodness of God and allow my faith in Him to carry me forward, even if I didn't have all the answers.

I recently learned through researching the teachings of Andrew Womack, founder of Charis Bible College, that for him, the question of God visiting blindness on that man need not even come up as we know that God wants good for all His children. In this view, the man was likely just born blind because we live in a broken world (broken by sin), and that Jesus just took advantage of the opportunity to care for this man and use it as a teaching opportunity at the same time. Even Matthew Henry often pointed out that Christ, having loved us first, often *saw* people. This man was just a blind beggar, likely an annoyance to many who wished not to be bothered, but Jesus saw the man and had compassion for him. Jesus picked him out of the crowd and chose to go to him.

Either way, whether the man was born blind according to the purposes of God or not, God, in His omniscience, wasn't surprised the man was there but, through pre-knowledge, had a plan. God's glory was made known in this man.

As I pondered the interaction of the man born blind and Christ, I thought of the thousands of people that had prayed for my wife to be healed throughout most of her life. I thought of the hundreds of occasions when one or more people had laid hands on her and prayed (James 5:14-15). I knew we both believed in the healing power of God and had seen and literally felt that particular miracle that I mentioned earlier. So, despite the potential accusations of some, I can't believe it was a lack of faith or a lack of acceptance of the miracle.

There is a teaching that God will always heal if there is faith and another that the healing is already done through the sacrifice of Christ; we must simply accept it. Proponents of either of these beliefs may very rightly claim that I am simplifying or misquoting them. But I believe I have the essence of these teachings down. If I follow either of these teachings, then I have to question my wife and even myself. Do we just not have enough faith, or are we belittling the work of grace on the cross? I cannot be more firm in my assurance that neither is the case!

As I continued to ponder the man born blind, in my pain and frustration, I would literally ask God, "How much glory do you need?" Seriously, not only would all the people present be blessed if my wife were to get up out of her wheelchair and walk, but much like those from many stories in the Gospels, we would be unable to stay quiet about the miracle! And I can only imagine that everywhere we went, people that we knew would stop us and ask questions, and the believers, and maybe some that weren't, would stop and glorify God. "How much glory do You need? When is her suffering enough?"

Like earlier, I never questioned God's love, but here I was, stuck, living with this question. And we continued to hear on a regular basis how inspiring we were or how inspiring our story was. This could be so awkward. We needed to boast in our weakness. We had to find a way to try to bring the praise back to God and not us.

This concept of boasting in our weakness comes from the teachings of the apostle Paul. In 2 Corinthians 12:7-10, Paul tells the church at Corinth that he had some sort of irritation. We don't know if it was a physical ailment or some other annoyance, but we know that it was severe enough that he attributed it to being a messenger of Satan. And he believed this suffering was given to him to keep him from exalting himself.

"You're such an inspiration." "It's amazing how you always have such a bright smile despite all you're going through." (Only ever said to my wife!) "How can I not be grateful when I look at you two?" The list goes on and on. On the one hand, we were so very grateful and usually amazed that God was using us, but these people only saw the good parts. They only saw my wife's excellent brave face. They had no idea that there was no question in my mind that He would care for us, but it drove me crazy never knowing how! And it seemed that over time, the answers took longer and longer to come. I even counted, I think 5 things that I'm waiting for the answers on right now, and I know that God will be completely in charge of at least three of them. So simultaneously, we would try to be gracious while screaming on the inside, "Oh yeah? Just come over at night when all we have is tears!" What people saw was His strength in the midst of our weakness.

We KNOW that our story has blessed and inspired people. It's a fact that's been repeated to us over and over again. But just saying it sounds so arrogant. The only truth is that we could never be those inspiring people without God! You have to live it to understand it. But it's a truth. When we lean on Him, sometimes not having any words to pray, all we can do is wail, "Oh God!" He is there. Those are the moments when we are forced to be so weak that only He can be strong. (Rom 8:26)

The idea of being weak so that He can be strong ties closely to other admissions that Paul makes. The end of Romans 7 and beginning of Romans 8 show Paul admitting that he can't manage to do the right things. He always picks idiotic things even though he knows better. But that's not what He wants! He wants to serve God! So he knows that the only answer is to look to the Spirit and LEAN IN! That's the best way I've ever been able to explain it to people.

Over the years, I've had to advocate for my wife in healthcare settings. This means that I watch the details, and I make sure that she gets the proper care. As in any profession, unfortunately, people make mistakes. A number of years ago, my wife was sent from a physical rehab hospital to another for some diagnostic testing as she was in extreme pain that didn't make sense to her doctors. A couple of days later, the sending hospital called me at work and asked if I knew where my wife was! Then they explained that they hadn't seen her in 48 hours since they sent her for diagnostic testing!

I made the 7-hour drive from where I worked to where she was hospitalized in probably much less. Now before I go any further, did I have the right to be upset? YES. While driving, I called the hospital where she had been sent for diagnostic testing, and sure enough, she was admitted as a patient. If she was in so much pain that they would have used an ambulance to send her to another hospital requesting diagnostic testing, she undoubtedly would have signed anything they put in front of her, including admission forms, and never known the difference. After all, she was so medicated that she couldn't make good decisions.

When I got to the nurse's station at the hospital it was very late, and they were only running the essential staff. I got to the counter and waited for what felt like long enough, even though it was probably nearly instantaneous. Then I started banging on the counter as loud as I could until a nurse came running. I said (probably too firmly), "I'm getting my wife dressed and taking her back to the hospital where she's supposed to be admitted. If you want me to sign any paperwork, it better be here when I get back, or it won't get signed!"

A moment later, as I was getting her dressed and packed to go, I heard jingling behind me. There were two police officers playing with their handcuffs. I had the right to be angry, but my behavior was not, shall we say, socially acceptable. The night ended without any further incident, and she ended up where she should be, and I drove two hours to our home. I tell this story because that is me. That's the natural, fleshly me. That's not me LEANING IN!

In comparison, over the last few years, there have been several more surgeries, two of them botched, which caused months of hospitalization as they tried to save her, then stabilize her. In all this time, nearly a year total, there have been humans, and human behaviors or priorities placed other than where I thought they should be as I watched her lying there on the brink of death. This time though, I learned the chain of command and politely and kindly addressed my concerns. In one instance, I did follow a young resident down the hall, arguing with him as to whether or not they were going to do a specific test, and he just wanted to get away. But I was still kind about it, he just didn't know what to do. His supervising doctor should have been the one that came to the room, and I'm sure that young resident learned from the experience.

But, instead of meeting the police, I made friends. I made allies. I developed relationships where I could go with concerns and needs. The difference this time was the harder it got, the harder I leaned into the Spirit. I might have told God, "I can't do this; this one's on You," as I dialed the phone or rolled my wheelchair down the hall.

The same Spirit that Paul talks about in the beginning of Romans 8 is the same Spirit that already knows our hearts AND the heart of God and prays for us when we can't find the words. (Sometimes we have words, but they sure aren't the right ones!) It's all the same good God, always and forever.

Supplicating with thankfulness

My wife had two spine surgeries a week apart, and the surgeons told us, "We know you need one more, but we want to let your body heal first." Over the next couple of days, though, we saw signs that they probably shouldn't wait. For example, as she was using a walker during physical therapy, the therapist was watching her feet. I was watching her hands as I rolled along next to her. The further she walked the more fingers let go of the walker, until I stopped her and the therapist and showed them. The doctors agreed with the need, but still wanted to be conservative. They booked the operating room for the following Monday morning and told us, "You have from now until the surgery time to make a decision." I had to come home for a few days and went back for the weekend. But we agreed that when I was there for the weekend, we wanted the decision to be behind us so that we could just enjoy being together.

The night before I headed back up, I called her. We had the same discussion we'd had repeatedly with the same pros and cons. But we knew we had to make a decision and had both been praying about it. Finally, she asked, "OK, enough. What do you think?" I told her we should do it. "Me too," she said. After our normal lovey dovey goodbye, we hung up. As I was sitting there on my deck chair, I realized that this would be surgery number 25 since we'd been married. I know a touch about statistics. I know that there is always a small risk that when you go into surgery, you might not make it. But it hit me that a small chance multiplied by 25 is a much bigger chance. I dropped my phone onto my chest as this hit me, and it felt like a huge boulder crushing me. Every single surgery she has increases the odds against us.

I went to Biblical advice that I teach so many of my counselees. It comes from Philippians 4:6-7. First, there is a plain instruction to not let anything make you anxious. But that boulder I felt on my chest was pure anxiety! Then it goes about a step by step plan, if you will, to shed anxiety. I don't know what word your favorite translation uses, but several say, "by prayer and supplication." OK, prayer is talking to God essentially. But what is supplication? The concept is so foreign to our modern minds. But anyone living several hundred years before and after this was written would have known exactly what this meant.

Living with authoritarianism

If we go back to the book of Esther, we see this in action. Whether you were living near your king or were in an occupied land like Israel when this was written, the leader over you was untouchable and unreachable. Even Queen Esther protested when she was told by Mordecai that she must approach the king to save all the Jews. This was obviously a cause dear to her heart as she was Jewish herself. But she knew that without the king's explicit permission, entering the throne room would bring a quick death. Even in the United States, trying to get to the president is, at best, ill-advised. There are any number of armed people between the average citizen and the Oval Office, for example.

This protection of the leader, whatever their title, created not only a safety net for them but it added to the separation between them and all of us peons. In many of these cultures, though, there were festivals where the king would allow the common folk to come with their needs and ask that they be met.

Imagine that you are a cabbage farmer. The fall and winter rains have given you the biggest harvest you've ever seen. How wonderful! But those same rains washed out the only road to the market. If you can't get your crop to the market, it will rot in your wagon, and your family will starve.

So, at the festival time, you walk to the castle and get in line with many others. To show your gratitude for being seen (thankfulness comes next in our verse), you brought the biggest bag of cabbage you can carry after picking through them to make sure they are the very best you could find. As the line enters the actual castle, you begin to feel the weight of where you are. As you get closer to the throne room, you can see that guards are heavily armed and only allowing one person in at a time. Then you're next in line. The guards tower over you, and their muscles bulge. But even more intimidating is that very sharp blade just inches from your face that is out there to remind you to mind your manners now and in the throne room.

As you are allowed to turn the corner and see into the throne room, you are awed by the splendor. You want to look around, but one ugly stare brings you back to the moment at hand. You bow so low; it's hard to walk. You only glance up long enough to see where you are going. Do you even dare look at the king?

This long walk is supplication. It is, in essence, reminding you that when you take a request before the Lord, He is God, and you aren't! It's a call to the appropriate humility. This is also where "Fear of the Lord" might come in handy. I know full well that I have fallen well short of His expectations. Thus, I should fear. But here's the beauty of it: He knows, but through the sacrifice of Jesus Christ, I am cleansed and safe from harm here in the throne room as I make my request.

This supplication is not just fear and reverence. It also brings hope. Go back to the cabbage farmer. Here you are in front of the only entity that has the power and resources, and authority to fix the road or, better yet, build a bridge. You have a chance to ask the only right person to help solve your problem and allow you to feed your family this year.

Then there is also that matter of thanksgiving. As the cabbage farmer, you are bringing a hopeful gift of the best you have to offer. This is where our example falls down a little bit. There is a group of Christians that say that you should be thankful for whatever you ask for because you know God is going to do it. Sorry, that's not me. I can't see God in that light.

If we go back to the previous chapter, I was hurting over the weight of the increased likelihood that my wife might not make it through surgery. So, as I remembered that God was God and I wasn't, I remembered that He loved her even more than I did and would do whatever was best. I told Him I trusted Him for that even though I wasn't ready to lose her. If that was how He would take away her pain, I would accept it. As the tears streamed down my face, I thanked Him for all the years we had together, and I saw her face.

That passage goes on to say that He will protect our hearts and minds with a peace that is incomprehensible. Through the power of Christ, in situations where the flesh can't even imagine being at peace, He will protect our hearts and minds by bringing it.

I got up to the hospital Saturday morning, and we talked and played cards, and I watched as she did her physical therapy. Then on Sunday, we read my daily devotions together and talked about what we heard God saying in those passages. Then I crawled in next to her in the hospital bed as we watched our favorite football team play on the hospital television.

Monday came, and I met the transport team downstairs and followed them into pre-op. I sat with her as all the doctors were coming through and the nurses were getting her ready. Then as it was time to wheel her back, we prayed and kissed. I went to the waiting room, and she went to the operating room, where she asked the staff in there if anybody wanted to join her in prayer.

According to all human sense (whether common or not), it would be expected for me to be consumed by anxiety during the surgery. Similar to previous surgeries my wife underwent, I should have been pacing the halls, desperately craving a sandwich, yet unable to stomach a bite due to the knots in my stomach. However, surprisingly, I found myself engrossed in the task of transferring data for my counseling ministry to a new system. The process was monotonous, and I struggled to stay awake on a few occasions. As I glanced up at the clock, it struck precisely the 1 ½ hour mark, which coincided with the anticipated duration of the surgery. I promptly began packing up my computer and gathering the various items scattered across the table in front of me. I rolled my wheelchair to a vantage point where I could observe the doctor's approach. I was well acquainted with the routine. If she emerged from the door on the left, it signified the recovery area and signaled good news. Conversely, if she exited through the door on the right, it meant proceeding to the consultation room where families were taken for difficult news. I got out my phone to play a game while I waited. Sure enough, she emerged through the door on the left.

The point is, I had gone before the throne with my prayer and supplication and thanksgiving. Now, I was protected by a peace that made no sense to my human brain.

She spent weeks in the Physical Therapy Rehab Unit, and we looked forward to her expected discharge date which was shortly before my cousin's wedding, and she was determined to dance with me. The therapists were cautiously optimistic or at least hid their doubts as they helped her along. And we did dance. It was more of a stand and wobble, but for us, it was the first dance in a very long time. Only recently, three years later, did she notice in the photographs that much of the dance floor emptied as people gathered around to watch.

But back home, as the giddiness wore off, the pain from the need for the next two surgeries began to set in. And the tear-filled late nights came back. People gathering around her in prayer for healing came back, too, as did all the people telling us how big an inspiration we were.

As time went on, I still wondered just how much glory did God need to receive, and I continued to try to plead and bargain despite knowing that wouldn't work. But something else began to happen too. It began to finally set in that the lives we led were bringing glory to God. I couldn't make sense of it, but it became clear that it wasn't just that people were inspired but that they were moved by and toward God.

Almost a year before this writing, my wife and I started down a path that looked like it should bring lots of hope. Instead, it brought months of challenge. My wife was hospitalized for roughly six months, and even after she was home, I was giving her three IV infusions a day, and a nurse came in weekly to check the IV site and draw blood for labs. This continued for several weeks. Everything she went through left her confused and frustrated. Once again, I laid next to her at night and wished God would let me in on the plan because this just wasn't working for me.

I love the book of Job. Job, like Abraham, knows how to talk about and to God. He speaks about and honors God's nature and who God is. But finally, Job begins to wonder, like I did when I asked, "How much glory do You need anyway?" In Job chapter 13, he finally asks why God is hiding His face and treating Job like an enemy. Both Job and I did the same thing, as I know many others do. The pain and frustration that we felt in the flesh finally overcame the truths we know of God in our spirits. As Paul talks about the battle between the flesh and the Spirit in Romans 7 and 8, this was one case where for both Job and me, the flesh finally won.

God began His response to Job in chapter 38. I'm going to give my very short and modernized version. "Job, pull up your big boy pants and consider this: Which mountain did you make anyway?"

When the flesh took over from the Spirit, we forgot our place a little bit, didn't we? Job forgot God's nature and challenged Him. "Why are You treating me like an enemy? What's up with that?" In reality, I'm sure that it is no different than my asking how much glory He needed. I was assuming that I knew the plan enough to know what He was after. Job and I both got a little full of ourselves.

Finally, He spoke to me. I guess I feel grateful that I didn't get the earful that Job did. Instead, I just heard one word, "Pots." I knew then exactly what God was saying to me.

In Romans 9, Paul is hurting over the jealousy of some of the Jewish Christians. In some of their minds, Christ was for them and not the Gentiles. He went on to remind them that actually, God was increasing the family He promised to Isaac by bringing in adopted sons too. This should have been a good thing.

He continued on to talk about how God hardened the hearts of some toward Him. I have a hard time with the prime example he referred to, the Pharaoh who watched his country be destroyed by plague after plague. It sounds like he didn't have some degree of free will. God told Pharaoh that He raised him up to demonstrate His power and make His name known. I don't pretend to understand the mind of God, and in the end, I'm not quite sure how this worked.

The passage goes on to ask what right the pot has to ask the potter for what use he is being made. One might be made to be a ceremonial goblet. Another might be made for some more utilitarian purpose. Believe it or not, I suddenly saw the glory in the ashes! I realized that we were completely in God's Sovereign Will. And as we live, our lives through our weakness are bringing Glory to God. Much like Matthew Henry wrote, we need to rejoice in being used to bring Him Glory.

Another example of the same idea might help. From the time I'm writing this, it is only a few days from a decade since my mother passed. She had what is normally an easily treatable cancer. I've had it myself. You can't even see the scar from where it was removed as it fits nicely into one of my wrinkles. However, because of the way my mother's cancer developed, the local oncologist sent us to a specialist in the nearest big town. I believe there are at least two trauma rated emergency rooms there as opposed to our local hospital, which has ONE surgeon on call.

After a couple of months in the hospital, my mom called and said she wanted to come home. So, I called the doctor and asked some very deliberate questions. He told me that they couldn't treat the cancer until they could heal up her surgical wounds. But it was almost a certainty that they couldn't get the surgical wounds to heal before the cancer killed her. Since the hospital in our hometown was considered a step-down, transferring her was something he didn't want to do. But I read between the lines that he was saying she was certainly going to die.

When I finally got her transferred to our hometown, I got a call from a nurse that had been a military medic in Iraq. When he saw my mother's condition, he said, "We don't even treat our enemies this badly." Looking back, I suspect that what he was really seeing was that the cancer was just so aggressive and so damaging that there was nothing the doctors could do to keep up. But what he said fueled my frustration and anger that in the middle of cancer treatments, nobody noticed that she was getting worse, not better. I wanted to start a malpractice case. When I told my mother, she simply said, "God knew. He knew."

I admit that, at the time, I had no idea what she meant. I couldn't be sure if what she was saying was profound or the effects of delirium. But I'm now sure that she was reminding me that God already knew what was going on, and as much as she wanted to stay around to minister, she was OK with whatever God had in mind. God knew. What my mom saw at that time was that she was in the palm of God's hand. Whether or not a surgeon or hospital failed to properly care for my mother was a small thing when compared to the beauty of knowing full well that you are in the palm of God's hand! (John 10:28-29, Isaiah 41:10, Isaiah 49:16)

We finally have caregivers helping out in the home. This is nice, but for two introverts who have been used to being alone, usually in our bedroom, for a couple of years, this is taking some adjustment. The house is cleaner than it has been in a long time, and there are many more cooked meals than we had become accustomed to. I do less and suffer from less pain and exhaustion than I have for a while.

With the extra help, we've been able to make it out of the door and to church. More and more people just fawn over my wife. And we hear more talk about how brave she is or how impressive our faith is. And we have to redirect when possible because we know us; she hates the pain, and I get angry. That's the flesh. That's who we are. But I've found that recognizing my weakness, and not just suffering, but acknowledging my weakness then leaning in,—allowing Him to be strong—gives us that something that people see.

I need to emphasize here, that I have learned through personal experience the power of acknowledging our hurts. Be they physical pain or emotional, we often don't have words for what we're feeling, we are just suffering. Sometimes this is because we don't want to feel the pain so we "stuff it." Whatever the reason, the pain that stays inside us is no more pleasant than a science experiment left in the back of the fridge. As it sits, it festers and grows, much like anger. But, if we stop for just a second and figure out what it is that is bothering us, we can then put it into words and acknowledge it.

When I was counseling in my office, given to me by a local church, if I was having a bad pain day, I would walk down the hall and tell the senior pastor. Then as soon as I acknowledged it, I could let it go as a weakness and let God be strong for me. Verbalizing it isn't a requirement, but for me it made the process easier. I recommend that you try that tactic, that you go to the same one or two people, making sure that they know you are not whining or complaining but just acknowledging so you can move on with His power. This is the meaning behind the oft misquoted Philippians 4:13, "I can do all things through Christ who strengthens me."[1] This verse is specifically talking about being able to live through any circumstance through Christ's strength.

All this talk about letting God be strong makes it sound easy. It usually isn't. This is where "bottom of the barrel" moments are handy. Whether it is changing our behaviors or it is not knowing how to pray, or it is something like a period of suffering, we have to be willing *to* be vulnerable. We have to be willing to be real. Whether it's the fact that we have very little true suffering in most of our lives, so we're not used to it, or maybe we wallow in our suffering. Whatever the reason may be, we have a tendency to get stuck there.

As a counselor, people don't come to me when problems begin to show up. No, they come to me when the problem has brought them to a crisis point. Very often, part of the reason is that people feel vulnerable when pouring out their hearts to a complete stranger. I feel like when we understand the enormity of God and His ability to see everything in us, it makes us feel even more vulnerable. We desire to hide even more.

At the beginning of Psalm 139, David declares that God sees everything he does. God even knows what word will come out of his mouth before it is on David's tongue. In verses 17 and 18, he recognizes that God thinks about him (David). So, although there is nowhere I can go to hide (I like my privacy!), the attention is nothing but loving. As David points out in this Psalm, realizing the difference and distance between who I am and who God is can be flat scary. There is no privacy, no secrets kept when it comes to God. This is often a roadblock for us.

There is no person on this planet that knows everything I'm thinking. I have learned that as a Christian minister, it is very important to have someone in my life whom I can trust and that loves me enough to be discreet AND real with me. I always keep at least one of those people in my life. Of course there is my dear wife. But beyond her and sometimes instead of her, the one I use the most is my friend, Charlie. He's not a family member, so he's not going to take things personally. He knows how I think and that I try to keep my focus right. He'll hear me say something that shows I'm slipping in my thought life in some area, and in his unique way, I can hear the smile in his voice as he says to me, "What was that? Say that again?" BUT, if I want to keep something from Charlie, I just don't call him. It's that easy. He's a busy guy. He knows I'm often very busy. So, there's no surprise or worry. He just figures I'll call when I need to. Now, I try not to keep secrets from Charlie. If I'm questioning a decision at all, he gets a text or a call, and we talk it through. But I CAN hide from Charlie. I CAN'T hide from God.

As Christians, we use the word omniscient to describe God. That means that He knows everything. But more than that, He sees all of us, and everything, and all time at the same time. God will never say, "Wow, I didn't see that coming!"

So, this vulnerability thing... the sooner we get over it, the better off we are. The more we realize that He isn't the National Security Agency listening in on our calls or something, but He's the Creator of all and thinks about us, the more we will be able to not just accept it but rejoice in it. Back to Romans 8:26-27, which says that when we don't know what to pray that the Spirit will intercede for us. If we understand the Spirit properly, we know that the Spirit knows our minds, and the Spirit knows God's mind. Who better to intercede than that?

Sometimes we try to block that out. And God will let us. You still can't surprise Him, but the Spirit won't force His way in to intercede for you. You need to accept that. I have on more than one occasion cried out, "Oh God!" then let myself break down into tears. I knew the Spirit was present and acting on my behalf. It was greatly comforting to know!

So yes, we can, to a degree, block the movement of the Spirit in our hearts, but why?! We need to go back to supplicating and remembering that God is God, and I'm not!

From the time of this writing, a surgery is scheduled for three weeks away. This will now be the 35th since we got married. Neither one of us is excited about the prospect of her having yet another surgery. But we know it is needed and, in all likelihood, will bring healing and relief from much of her pain.

Thinking about the upcoming surgery, believe me, neither my wife nor I want to load up the van with the supplies to help her be comfortable and safe in a hotel room bed. Neither of us wants her to go under anesthesia and have a room of imperfect humans cutting her open. WE DO NOT WANT IT! Knowing it is what is best for her unless God intervenes in the meantime, we will move forward. I have no choice but to give the finances for this trip and the very life of my bride over to Him. OK, I have a choice. But what kind of a choice is it?

Whatever happens that day, even if I come home alone, I know that God already knew. He thinks of me, but at the moment, most importantly, He thinks of her constantly. He cares about her more than I can. So, as I enter the throne room, humbly and with thanks for what I already have been given, I can face the uncertain future with peace that doesn't even make sense to me.

And during the healing or grieving process, I can sit in the ashes in pain. But all the while, there is glory there! He has chosen me for this purpose, and somehow people are inspired and moved toward God through our lives and my life. If I serve no other purpose on this planet, that is purpose enough! I will accept being whatever the potter chose to make me. And I will choose to wait for the Glory to become evident as I do.

Y ou don't have to be miserable even if you feel like you are living in the ashes of your life. As a counselor, I've come to realize that almost everyone has something that haunts them. As you've read much of my story, you may very well have read parts that reminded you a little too much of your own pains.

There's nothing unique or special about me, not in comparison to you. God made us both. I have no idea who or how He made you. But I do know He made you to be you on purpose (Psalm 139). He knitted you together in your mother's womb! He put in you a unique set of skills and traits that nobody has in the exact same combination. And He gave you a specific temperament, which is essentially the root of personality. You can change your personality, but you can't change who God made you to be.

But the problem is that we live in a broken world, and bad things happen that are not of God's design. For most of us, those things we have lived through have combined with our inborn temperament and caused us problems. In some extreme cases, that goes as far as severe personality disorders. For most of us, these personality traits just make our lives and the lives of the people we care about, a little harder. For me, it was an attitude that I didn't want to deal with people, and that often turned into anger. We can live in that. I did for many years. If nothing else, though, that's really not much fun. At worst, we leave a wake of destruction behind us (which I feel like I did for many years). But we know that God will use all things in some way for our good (Romans 8:28). This doesn't mean that everything is good! It means that either something will come along that the garbage prepares us for, or maybe we will become people that can help others out of their muck and mire. You don't need to be a trained professional counselor to come alongside someone and be an example for them as you listen and care.

How do you get there, though? Well, that's why I spent all the previous pages being sometimes painfully transparent. Because I wanted to show you first that the changes can come and secondly what the steps look like.

If you haven't yet, please accept the gift that the Creator of all wants to give you. He wants to remove the blame of your failings through the death of Jesus Christ on the cross. He is standing at the door of your Heart and knocking. All you have to do is let Him in. Eternal forgiveness is free, It's a gift. I once had a sermon illustration where I called people up and handed them a beautifully wrapped box and said, "Christ was born and died to give you this gift of freedom from sin." (They each had an action and a line they were supposed to say and most got it wrong and hilarity ensued. But the point was made.)

Find a local church and ask questions of the leadership there. Find a church where you can be comfortable and call it home. Then I strongly suggest you get baptized to declare you are a new person.

If you already have done that, then the next step is simple, even if it feels difficult at first. Go to the throne room and humbly make your requests known. Remember that humility is remembering that He is God and you are not. That calls for humility but is a good thing because remember, He is the one that has all the resources and ability to heal your heart. And don't forget to find something to thank Him for.

Next, work on accepting the vulnerability. Learn to embrace His constant love for you and presence with you. Work toward that being a relief, not an intrusion. When you are at your end and don't even know what to say, just cry out to Him and let the Spirit in to intercede on your behalf.

And look for the glory that God receives through who He made you to be. "For through the grace given to me I say to everyone among you not to think more highly of himself than he ought to think; but to think so as to have sound judgment, as God has allotted to each a measure of faith."[1] (Romans 12:3). This one seems harder than it is. The beginning of the verse is pretty obvious. But this verse is also helpful for those that can't believe they have value. Not only did God create you specifically and deliberately, but He also has characteristics, skills, and traits that He sees in you that maybe you don't. It's easy to get blinded by the ashes. It's hard to think with "sound judgment" when all we can see is pain. But God already has His vision of you available for you. It may take prayer and time to see it, but the verse says that "He has allotted to each a measure of faith." That's present perfect tense. That means it was done and still is done! As you begin to see what He sees in and for you, then you will be more able to see how you are in His hand. Try making a list of what you think He sees in you. Then pray over it and go back through it. Go from things you do to things he made you to be. You want traits not actions. And remember, these are the things that God sees, because He put them there. That doesn't mean you're living in them, nor does it mean that God made you to be the things that you are living. It will likely take several runs at the list trying to drill down to the core trait before you get there. You may even find things that you aren't. That's not a bad thing, it's realistic. I put on a charity event every year and the people that come frequently tell me how much they look forward to it and some ask me to consider doing it twice a year. I can put the event on and make it very entertaining. But I don't get involved in the small talk amongst the participants. That's too much and not at all who I am. I know that and I don't try to be that because that's not who God made me to be.

But as you learn who you really are in Him and find His love for you then you can begin to really see that you are indeed in His hand. He still won't put everything together the way that you imagine or want. But if you know that you are His and He knows everything about you including your future then you can begin to trust Him even when life isn't much fun. And as you do, you will begin to see His glory in the ashes.

It is my belief, and the belief of all the people that supported this project and others, that this is a message that needs to be spread far and wide. If you got something from this book or if you agree that it is an important message that needs to be spread, I need your help! Please take the time to write a good review wherever you bought this (Reviews drive visibility). Please share with others how much you enjoyed the book.

Also, I'd love for you to sign up to receive 30 Inspirational Memes in 30 Days at https://revmatthewhogan.com/get-30-inspirational-memes-in-30-days/

If you'd like a primer on beating anxiety, you can get my free short eBook at Beating Anxiety Biblically[1]

---

1.   https://revmatthewhogan.com/beating-anxiety-biblically/

Bibliography

1. Scripture quotations are taken from the (NASB®) New American Standard Bible®, Copyright © 1960, 1971, 1977, 1995 by The Lockman Foundation. Used by permission. All rights reserved. www.lockman.org[1]

2. Shriners clubs are a charitable fraternity, much like Lions clubs or Rotary clubs. The Shriners support the Shriner's Childrens Hospitals. They're not as well known as possibly St. Judes, but they are as important. Most people know the Shriners as the men on mini bikes or little clown cars wearing red fezzes in parades.

3. The Allies were a Christian rock band recording albums from 1985 to 1995. The best known member of the band was their singer, Bob Carlisle, who released the daddy-daughter song "Butterfly Kisses" as a solo project.

---

1. http://www.lockman.org

Don't miss out!

Visit the website below and you can sign up to receive emails whenever Reverend Matthew Hogan publishes a new book. There's no charge and no obligation.

https://books2read.com/r/B-A-PQWAB-VVBPC

BOOKS 2 READ

Connecting independent readers to independent writers.

About the Author

Reverend Matthew Hogan has over 30 years of experience in ministry and counseling, having worked as a pastor, interim pastor, and counselor. He is a Certified Temperament Pastoral Counselor, Licensed Clinical Pastoral Counselor, as a Clinical Professional member of the National Christian Counselors Association. Currently, he runs Grace for Individual and Family Therapy (GIFT) through which he provides faith-based therapy for individual clients, couples, and groups of any faith background online.

A lifelong motorcycle enthusiast, Matthew is also the founder of Rods N' Rides, through which he runs motorcycle events that raise money for charity. Rods N' Rides donates the money it raises to the Pediatric Brain Tumor Foundation, inspired by Matthew's late brother-in-law, who was a pediatric brain tumor survivor. He also participates in the Tour of Honor, a multi-state motorcycling event in which riders visit different monuments and memorials throughout the country, raising funds for veterans, police, and firefighters. Matthew enjoys spending time on his motorcycle communing with God, and experiencing the country's many unique sights.

Matthew is the proud husband of Kimberly Hogan and father to their adult daughter, Emily. Kimberly and Matthew met when Matthew was enrolled in Central Christian College and shared a spontaneous first date at a horror movie before getting married 33 days later. They currently live together in Arizona with their four cats, who are all rescues.

Read more at https://revmatthewhogan.com/.